T0005550

To all young readers,
in honor of the books they dare to love
—B.K.

This book is for Jack.
—C.B.

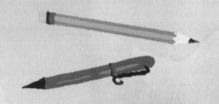

Text copyright © 2023 by Beth Kephart
Jacket art and interior illustrations copyright © 2023 by Chloe Bristol

All rights reserved. Published in the United States by Anne Schwartz Books,
an imprint of Random House Children's Books,
a division of Penguin Random House LLC, New York.

Anne Schwartz Books and the colophon are trademarks of Penguin Random House LLC.

Selected text from *Dear Genius* by Leonard S. Marcus. COPYRIGHT © 1998 BY LEONARD MARCUS.
Used by permission of HarperCollins Publishers.
Photo of Ursula Nordstrom copyright © Erich Hartmann/Magnum Photos.

Visit us on the Web! rhcbooks.com

Educators and librarians, for a variety of teaching tools, visit us at RHTeachersLibrarians.com

Library of Congress Cataloging-in-Publication Data is available upon request.
ISBN 978-0-593-37957-8 (trade) — ISBN 978-0-593-37958-5 (lib. bdg.) — ISBN 978-0-593-37959-2 (ebook)

The text of this book is set in 15-point IM FELL DW Pica Pro.
The illustrations were rendered digitally in Adobe Photoshop.
Book design by Nicole de las Heras

MANUFACTURED IN CHINA

10 9 8 7 6 5 4 3 2 1

First Edition

Random House Children's Books supports
the First Amendment and celebrates the right to read.

GOOD BOOKS FOR BAD CHILDREN

· THE GENIUS OF URSULA NORDSTROM ·

WRITTEN BY
BETH KEPHART

ILLUSTRATED BY
CHLOE BRISTOL

a·s·b
anne schwartz books

Ursula Nordstrom
was a grown-up
who never forgot
what it was to be a child.

hibit
ou
d
to

ll thoug your
Book Week w imply
me of these a you
all your article
're not pretty near
n't been able to
, but I will make
as I remember.
speeches
or later

Her parents had been glamorous—
dashing Henry,
an actor, comedian, and magician;

gorgeous Marie,
an opera singer and actress.

No brother.
No sister.
Just Ursula,
who watched the world
and listened.

She heard the sound of her father's voice
as he read his favorite books out loud—
Nicholas Nickleby, David Copperfield.
"You must know books, learn books, love books," he'd tell her,
and turn the page.

She heard the sound
of her parents fighting.
Alone in her room,
Ursula would escape into the
adventures of Beatrix Potter.
She'd read *The Wonderful
Wizard of Oz*.
She'd turn the pages
of her own imagination.

Ursula was seven when her parents divorced.
Arrangements were made.
Her bags got packed.
She left New York City for Long Island
and a school called Winnwood.

Through the windows of her train,
she watched the smear of the world
and tried to imagine what was next.

At boarding school, Ursula slowly made friends.
She was funny, a spark—
a girl who laughed,
but who could also feel alone,
and different.

At sixteen, Ursula left Winnwood
for Northfield Seminary in Massachusetts,
where she was soon dreaming of college—
of a degree and a career
as a writer, maybe,
or a social worker.
But college was expensive.
Ursula would have to get a job instead.

And so she did.
In the College Textbook Department of
Harper & Brothers . . .

. . . she clerked, she filed, she typed.
Every day like the day before for
five
long
years.

And then, in the Harper cafeteria,
Ursula made a friend—
Ida Louise Raymond,
from the Department of Books for
Boys and Girls.
Louise.

"Would you be my assistant?"
Louise asked Ursula one day.
"Yes," Ursula said.

She answered the phone.
She read the manuscripts of
famous authors.
She read letters from children
who had loved the books
that she'd helped publish.

Every day was new,
an excellent education.

For four years, Ursula learned from Louise.
And then, when Louise left,
Ursula was promoted.
Louise's department became hers.

Now it was up to Ursula to choose
what kinds of
funny
naughty
scary
true
children's books
she might publish.

Up to her
to find the writers and artists
with the most terrific ideas.

the
RUNAWAY
BUNNY
Margaret Wise Brown
Art by Clement Hurd

THE ASTOR LIBRARY

LENOX LIBRARY

THE TILDEN TRUST

NEW YORK PUBLIC LIBRARY

Up to her
to talk to librarians, teachers, parents
about her favorite books of all—

good books for bad children,
as she liked to say.

"Come right in!" Ursula would shout
to those who showed up, unannounced.

"Come see me," she would insist
to those she discovered
in the pages of magazines.
"You've come home," she'd say.

"Answer that!" she'd yell at her assistant
when the phone would ring.
"That could be the next Mark Twain."

Ursula published what she pleased.
She was curious.
She was honest.
She knew what to ask her writers and artists
and how best to listen—
how to stare out through her bright blue eyes
and her wide spectacles
and encourage their most fabulous stories.

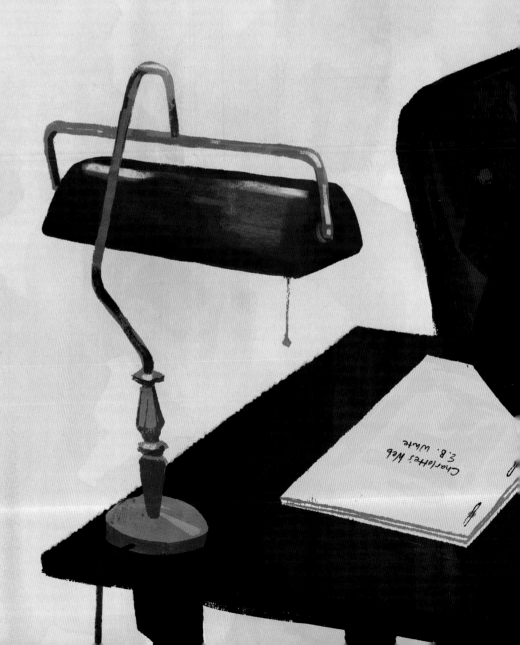

Charlotte's Web
E. B. White

"Children want to feel seen," she said,
in a voice some called musical
and some called gravelly.
"Children deserve our best."

Ursula demanded perfection from others.
"Not good enough for you,"
she would sometimes scribble to a writer
in the margins of a manuscript
she believed could be better.

"It does need pulling together,"
she wrote to Margaret Wise Brown
about a draft of *The Runaway Bunny*.

Ursula also demanded perfection from herself:
"I'm awfully sorry my first reaction to *Harold*
was so lukewarm. . . . I certainly was wrong,"
she apologized to Crockett Johnson,
for not liking *Harold and the Purple Crayon* early on.

Ursula clacked out her thoughts
on her noisy Smith Corona typewriter,
making mistakes and not stopping to fix them.

about it. But before we even
look at it I'm rushing this off
to you so I can enclose a page
from our catalogue for this
spring. It shows you a bit
about a Ruth Krauss book with
pictures by Maurice Sendak
called The Birthday Party.
I do hope that it isn't too
similar to yours, but I thought
that there is this remote
possibility. . . . I must say

RUTH KRAUSS
WESTPORT. CT

CONTACTS

Smith Corona

Dear Janice: I really can't keep on
with last minute. Is this all
right? Please call if you can.
if you can reach me, young the
older but lots of do the
world, but lots of useful lot of
people do you have terribly far
none so you have terribly far
sickness the work. I'm writing
since the we say not be
dear and Kind letter you about your
I'd like to write you promptly
my manuscript. We'll read it
quickly; What won't take any
time. takes time is thinking

URSULA NORDSTROM
HARPER & BROTHERS
NEW YORK, NY

Once, when the phone rang,
Ursula picked it up
and closed her eyes
and listened
as Margaret Wise Brown
read the first sentences of
her new story:

In the great
green room,

there was a telephone
and a red balloon. "

This would become *Goodnight Moon*.

When Ruth Krauss came to the office
and read from a pile of cards . . .

BUTTONS ARE TO KEEP
PEOPLE WARM!

RUGS ARE SO DOGS
HAVE NAPKINS
!!!

FACES ARE FOR
MAKING
FACES!

. . . Ursula laughed
until the seams of her rumpled suit split
and her jewelry jangled.
That was the start of *A Hole Is to Dig*.

Sometimes Ursula would find a way
to help her writers and artists end their stories.
Like when Maurice Sendak
came to her with a tale about a boy named Max
who goes on a wild stomp of an adventure.

The problem?
Maurice didn't know how to get Max back home.

"Well, why did Max want to go home?" Ursula asked and asked again.

"Well, he wanted to be where someone loved him best of all,

"Why not?" Ursula asked.

It was the perfect question,
which led to the perfect ending
for *Where the Wild Things Are*

Ursula would remind her writers to write what they knew: "And never forget that what you told me is something ONLY YOU know about," she wrote to John Steptoe, who was still a high school student when the two met to talk about his first book, *Stevie*.

And she would remind anyone who called stories
too naughty, funny, or scary
that there are all kinds of children who need all
kinds of books:

> books for children who feel sad
> books for children who get mad
> books for children who feel different
> books for children who are lonely
> books for children who have secrets

Once, when Ursula was asked
to explain why she, a grown-up
who had not gone to college,
who had never been a teacher or librarian,
had any business making books for children,
she declared:
"I am a former child, and I haven't forgotten a thing."

Ursula took care of her artists and writers—
her geniuses, as she called them.
They had names for her too—
Ursula Maelstrom
and Ursula Major—
and on October 23, 1951,
they held an Ursula Nordstrom Day,
filling her office with gifts and flowers and funny telegrams.

There were years upon years of an interesting life,
a meaningful, bold, and brave life,
though sometimes, still, the quiet slipped in,
late at night, when the moon was high
and it was just Ursula
in the office.

Decades went by.
At last Ursula retired
and headed home
to her quiet house in Connecticut,
where she lived with Mary Griffith,
the woman she loved.

Sometimes, when the colors changed,
and the school year began,
Ursula would remember
Winnwood,
and the train she had ridden,
and the smear of the windows,
and the child she had been.

And then she'd remember
all those good books for all those bad children.
The only proper kind of books,
in her opinion.

Author's Note

URSULA NORDSTROM (1910–1988) was a groundbreaking editor of children's books who had a very special gift for spotting and encouraging talent. Her relationships with writers and illustrators like Maurice Sendak, Margaret Wise Brown, E. B. White, Shel Silverstein, Ruth Krauss, John Steptoe, Crockett Johnson, Meindert DeJong, Louise Fitzhugh, and Else Holmelund Minarik generated a long list of classic books that we're still reading today.

Named director of Harper Books for Boys and Girls in 1940, Ursula went on to become the first woman elected to Harper & Company's board of directors and the first woman to become a Harper vice president and then a senior vice president. In 1973, she became a senior editor of Ursula Nordstrom Books; after that she was a consultant. Whatever her title, she was always Ursula—ferociously engaged, complicated, funny, demanding—a woman who called children "brand-new people" and who would sit at her desk, twisting and untwisting paper clips, talking and listening and thinking. She famously bought presents for her writers. Sometimes her writers bought her presents, too—like the big silver pendant she would wear around her neck, a gift from writer Mary Rodgers, and even a dog from Margret Rey.

Remembering her days at boarding school, Ursula wrote a novel herself. Titled *The Secret Language,* it begins: "Sooner or later everyone has to go away from home for the first time." Going away from home was a feeling Ursula never forgot, and so she worked as an editor to create an unwaveringly safe place for her writers and artists.

"I loved her on first meeting," said Maurice Sendak, who wrote books like *Where the Wild Things Are.* "My happiest memories, in fact, are of my earliest career, when Ursula was my confidante and best friend."

I fell in love with Nordstrom several years ago, when teaching children's literature at the University of Pennsylvania. In preparation for my first-day lecture, I reread Jill Lepore's 2008 *New Yorker* story called "The Lion and the Mouse: The Battle That Reshaped Children's Literature." There, in that story, was Ursula, proudly defending E. B. White's right to write about a talking mouse named Stuart Little. My kind of editor, I thought.

Everything else I read—including *Dear Genius: The Letters of Ursula Nordstrom*—further inflamed my passion for this woman who knew just what to say and when to say it, even if she was sometimes loud and sometimes defiant, sometimes sad and often mysterious, in her quest to create such good books for bad children. I have followed her through the channels of my own imagination—puzzling through her inconsistencies, weighing the mythologies, and doing my utmost best to honor her, with the help of my own perfection-nudging editor, Anne Schwartz. Many thanks, finally, to Crescent Dragonwagon and Fran Manushkin, who generously shared their memories of Ursula's world, and, of course, to Leonard S. Marcus, whose exquisite work on the Nordstrom letters and his own review of an early draft of this book were pivotal to the book's development.

Sources

Blewett, Kelly. "Reading Children's Book Editor Ursula Nordstrom: Archives of Literacy Sponsorship, Workplace Persuasion, and Queer Networks." *Peitho Journal* 20, no. 1, 2017.

Blewett, Kelly. "Ursula Nordstrom and the Queer History of the Children's Book." *Los Angeles Review of Books,* August 28, 2016.

Brown, Margaret Wise. Illustrated by Clement Hurd. *Goodnight Moon.* New York: HarperCollins, 1947.

Brown, Margaret Wise. Illustrated by Leonard Weisgard. *Night and Day.* New York: HarperCollins, 1942.

Brown, Margaret Wise. Illustrated by Clement Hurd. *The Runaway Bunny.* New York: HarperCollins, 1942.

Corsaro, Julie. "Nordstrom, Ursula." *Pioneers and Leaders in Library Services to Youth: A Biographical Dictionary.* Westport, CT: Libraries Unlimited, 2003.

Crichton, Sarah. "What We Read as Youngsters: Top Editors Recall Their Favorite Childhood Books." *Publishers Weekly,* February 26, 1982.

DeJong, Meindert. Illustrated by Maurice Sendak. *The Wheel on the School.* New York: HarperCollins, 1972.

Fitzhugh, Louise. *Harriet the Spy.* New York: Delacorte Press, 1964.

Hoff, Syd. *Danny and the Dinosaur.* New York: Puffin Books, 1983.

Krauss, Ruth. Illustrated by Crockett Johnson. *The Carrot Seed.* New York: HarperCollins, 1945.

Lee, MacKenzi. *Bygone Badass Broads: 52 Forgotten Women Who Changed the World.* New York: Abrams, 2018.

Marcus, Leonard S. "The UN Tapes." *The Horn Book Magazine* 84, no. 2, 2008.

Minarik, Else Holmelund. Illustrated by Maurice Sendak. *Little Bear.* New York: HarperCollins, 1957.

Natov, Roni, and Geraldine DeLuca. "Discovering Contemporary Classics: An Interview with Ursula Nordstrom." *The Lion and the Unicorn* 3, no. 1. Baltimore: Johns Hopkins University Press, 1979.

Nordstrom, Ursula. *Dear Genius: The Letters of Ursula Nordstrom,* edited by Leonard S. Marcus. New York: Harper Collins, 1998.

Nordstrom, Ursula. "Editing Books for Young People." In *Celebrating Children's Books: Essays on Children's Literature in Honor of Zena Sutherland,* edited by Betsy Hearne and Marilyn Kaye. New York: Lothrop, Lee and Shepard Books, 1981.

Nordstrom, Ursula. *The Secret Language.* New York: Harper Trophy, 1960.

Nordstrom, Ursula. "Some Thoughts on Children's Books in the United States." *Graphis* Special Issue: Children's Book Illustration 27, no. 155, 1971–72.

Sendak, Maurice. *In the Night Kitchen.* New York: HarperCollins, 1970.

White, E. B. Illustrated by Garth Williams. *The Annotated Charlotte's Web.* Annotations by Peter F. Neumeyer. New York: HarperCollins, 1994.

White, E. B. Illustrated by Garth Williams. *Stuart Little.* New York: HarperCollins, 1945.

Zion, Gene. Illustrated by Margaret Bloy Graham. *Harry the Dirty Dog.* New York: HarperCollins, 1956.

Zolotow, Charlotte. Illustrated by William Pène du Bois. *William's Doll.* New York: HarperCollins, 1972.

Multiple articles in *Publishers Weekly* also supported my research.

Illustration Note: The mustached man in Ursula's office is the author E. B. White.